BRITAIN'S HERITAGE

Brutalism

Billy Reading

AMBERLEY

Acknowledgements

The author and publisher would like to thank the following people/organisations for permission to use copyright material in this book:

Simon Reading: Images 13, 36, 67 and 54 & 55; Bob Giddings: Images 28 & 29; Sylvia Warman: Image 30; Georgina Watts: Image 78; Gary Fooks: Image 42; Ali Boon: Images 60 & 61; Andrea Perrot: Images 47, 48, 69 & 79; Kath Fall: Image 81; Getty Images: Images 2, 3, 7, 4, 9, 10, 15, 23, 25, 26, 31, 35, 37 & 38, 39, 49, 55, 56, 68, 70.

All other images are the author's own, or kindly supplied by Liz Reading.

Every attempt has been made to seek permission for copyright material used in this book. However, if we have inadvertently used copyright material without permission/acknowledgement we apologise and we will make the necessary correction at the first opportunity.
   In addition, the author would like to thank the following people: Richard Hurley, Liz Reading, Maude, Audrey, Tom Reading, Nick Wright, Simon Reading, Bob Giddings, Barbara Jacklin, Fiona Taylor, Sylvia Warman, Gary Fooks, Andrea Perrot, Ali Boon, Georgina Watts, Louise Platt, Linda Brown and Kath Fall.

To my Dad, for concrete, and my Mum, for Swansea Civic Centre (twice.)

First published 2018

Amberley Publishing
The Hill, Stroud
Gloucestershire, GL5 4EP

www.amberley-books.com

Copyright © Billy Reading, 2018

The right of Billy Reading to be identified as the Author of this work has been asserted in accordance with the Copyrights, Designs and Patents Act 1988.

ISBN 978 1 4456 7552 7 (paperback)
ISBN 978 1 4456 7553 4 (ebook)

British Library Cataloguing in Publication Data.
A catalogue record for this book is available from the British Library.

Printed in the UK.

Contents

Salters' Hall in the City of London, built in 1968 by the John S. Bonnington Partnership to an initial design concept by Basil Spence. The tooled concrete finish and dramatic massing contrast with an ancient section of Roman city wall.

1
Introduction

This book focuses on a movement in architectural history known as brutalism, which developed from the much larger, international architectural movement called modernism. Beginning in the early twentieth century, modernism was the defining style of its time and is characterised by buildings that express their function and reject decorative ornamentation, using the advancing technology of the period playfully and creatively to bring new materials and ideas into architecture. Deriving from modernism, brutalism began as an architectural theory in the late 1950s, expanding and evolving in the 1960s and '70s.

Fifty years on from its height, brutalism can be understood in the wider context of architectural history. However brutalism goes beyond history and theory, as through physical buildings that we use, it forms part of our lives and experiences as well as part of our towns and cities. For many, the invisible factors that created brutalist buildings and the extra layers of meaning that we attach to them still influence how we perceive them.

All architectural history is shaped by politics and socio-economics, and disentangling these influences can be a challenging business, especially when the emotive responses of the public to the architecture in question remain polarised. Architectural styles come and go, and fall in and out of favour. Each generation tends to reflect upon and react to the favoured style of the last with distaste. The subsequent generation then tend to champion the underdog, and so rally around the architecture that is under threat. In this way architecture, particularly experimental or cutting-edge architecture, is often loved, loathed and then loved again.

Brutalism is a loaded term. It is likely to garner a reaction, although the nature of that reaction could be wildly different depending on whom you are talking to. Many of the architects whose work we now consider as brutalist rejected the phrase. For some people, brutalist architecture is an honest expression of socialist ideals – equality in housing, access to the arts for all – architecture as a social leveller. In this view, brutalism is representative of a time when a generous welfare state was developing new models of social housing provision, civic and cultural centres, modern hospitals, free university places and more. A time – perhaps the last time – when architecture was innovative, creative and aspirational. The fact of these buildings being neglected and run-down during the latter twentieth century is seen by this audience as symptomatic of a political shift towards less generous state provision, and a conscious (and regrettable) move away from the utopian ideals, innovation and bravado of their architects.

On the opposing side, brutalism represents the architecture of dystopian failure – of cheapness in material and finish, vulgarity and absurdity of form and so monumentally overwhelming that it serves to isolate the individual. Here brutalist buildings represent the failed socialist ideals of a generation, indicative in the poor condition of grimy concrete. As such, the view is that these monstrous monuments to mid-twentieth-century socialism through architecture and urban planning should be resigned to the dustbin of history – we should accept that they failed, call them 'concrete monstrosities', sweep them away and start again.

This book is part of a series on Britain's heritage, introductory guides to the buildings, places, movements and ideas that have shaped our country. Writing an introductory guide to a complex movement in architectural history which combines politics, economics and architectural theory is a challenge. The scope of this book is to introduce the subject – to discover where and how it came about, which key buildings embody brutalism and why – which are the buildings, places and people that give rise to this extraordinary, distinctive and divisive style.

2
Brutal Beginnings

Twentieth-century architecture was dominated by modernism, which has also been called International Modern or International Style. Evolving and unfurling over many decades and various continents, modernism subsequently became an umbrella term for a whole host of derived architectural styles including Futurism, Constructivism and Bauhaus. Another of these many architectural derivations is brutalism. Understanding brutalism in Britain therefore begins with the sleek rectilinear volumes and open, light-filled spaces of modernism. A reaction against the past and an architecture for the machine age, early modernism was radical and progressive. The recognised champion of the style is the Swiss architect Le Corbusier.

In Britain this shockingly new style of the 1920s and '30s was initially treated with suspicion. Aside from a handful of small buildings and private commissions, pre-war or

Did you know?

Prolific Swiss architect Le Corbusier was born with the name Charles-Édouard Jeanneret-Gris in 1887, but renamed himself with an amended version of his grandfather's name in the 1920s. He is commonly referred to by many architects as 'Corb'.

Le Corbusier has been called the father of brutalism. His 1960s designs for 'units of living' and 'radiant cities' provided glimpses of what architecture and urban planning could be in the future. (Getty Images)

even interwar modernism is fairly rare in Britain. The British architectural establishment during these decades remained focused on seeking modernity through tradition, exemplified by pared-back classicism and the stripped neo-Georgian aesthetic, updating imperialist architectural styles that reinforced hierarchical social structures. The late nineteenth-century preoccupation with finding a modern architecture that drew on and updated the perceived English vernacular remained and Continental modernism was not seen as the solution.

Modernists famously stripped away the fussiness and decoration of generations of earlier architects, stating 'ornamentation is a crime!' and replacing classical decoration with sleek, sweeping clean lines. This was an approach fit for the machine age; buildings became efficient 'machines for living in'. The clean lines and revolutionary building materials were futuristic – looking forward to a less fussy, less structured society that was ready to turn its back on the past – rejecting social hierarchies, rejecting ornamentation, embracing the machine age and mass production; doing away with the coal-stained and soot-smoked red-brick architecture of the nineteenth century – particularly the gloomy gothic and all that this represented.

Some British architects were more open to these emerging new ideas. Also, European refugees who settled in Britain brought with them a greater appetite for modernism. Early British buildings that explored the expanding possibilities of materials and adopted the modernist aesthetic include the Isokon building in London by Wells Coates and the famous penguin pool at London Zoo by Berthold Lubetkin, both of 1934.

The sculptural ramps of Lubetkin's Penguin Pool at London Zoo were a revolution when designed in 1934. Sadly the penguins did not agree, and are today housed in a more natural habitat. (Getty Images)

Architect husband-and-wife team Peter and Alison Smithson, photographed here over their drawing boards in 1961. Peter Smithson later claimed the term brutalism was derived from his college nickname of Brutus. (Getty Images)

A significant channel through which European modernist approaches in architecture and urbanism were discussed, refined and shared was the Congrès Internationaux d'Architecture Moderne, commonly known by the abbreviation CIAM. This congress, centred in continental Europe, held its inaugural meeting in La Sarraz in Switzerland in 1928. Eminent architects including Le Corbusier were founding members. The congress met each summer and focused on a specific theme; for example 'the minimum dwelling' (CIAM II) or 'the functional city' (CIAM IV.)

From 1933 a linked group called the Modern Architecture Research Group (MARS) was established, strengthening connections between CIAM and modernist architects in the UK. After 1945, with a number of architects having emigrated during the war years, stronger links were forged between Britain, Europe and North America. In 1953, CIAM IX was held in Aix-en-Provence in France with the theme of 'habitat'. A number of architects from a younger generation than the founders discovered that they were increasingly dissatisfied with the radical functionalism of the 'elders' of the group. Increasing divisions between CIAM's founders and the group's younger members led eventually to a schism, and the foundation of Team Ten (or Team X). This group included British husband-and-wife architects Peter and Alison Smithson. The division persisted for the remaining years of CIAM, and ultimately contributed to the end of the organisation in 1959, when their last conference was held in Otterlo in the Netherlands.

The Second World War had changed Europe irrevocably, and art, architecture and engineering were no exception. Throughout the war, a new and pressing set of priorities re-shaped architectural thinking. Issues such as the speed and ease of construction, reduction of costs, blast resistance and de-mountability all propelled new ideas to the forefront, particularly around reinforced concrete and prefabrication. The lessons learnt during this priority shift in architecture stayed in the minds of British architects after 1945. Structures that had appeared in the landscape, for example the German gun emplacement in Guernsey, as well as British pill-boxes, aircraft hangars, bunkers and many other such structures of conflict would have seemed initially alien to established architecture and to the landscape. However, these materials and forms can be seen as a precursor to the shifts in architecture that influenced the post-war world.

Above and left: Structures of conflict; this German gun emplacement in Guernsey foretells many of the ideas that went on to shape post-war architecture in Europe. The shuttering marks in the close-up picture demonstrate how the structure was rapidly erected. These types of construction marks later went on to be used to artistic effect.

In early 1950s Britain a massive rebuilding programme was required: housing, transport, infrastructure and industrial design – everything was set to change. A number of elements fell into place which combined to transform how buildings were built, what they looked like and what was expected of them. A rapid population increase, a boom in cheap energy, the increase in car ownership and in air travel, the creation of the National Health Service, even the reaction to continued shortages and rationing of traditional building materials and labour skills; all of these factors necessitated and contributed to a revolution in the construction industry.

The public's expectations of buildings began to shift. The old, cold, damaged terraced housing of the Victorian and Georgian periods was not just disliked but hated – blamed for a whole host of problems; indicative of the enshrined social injustice of the pre-war world and therefore considered corrosive to society, detrimental to physical and mental health and worthy only for the bulldozer. Swathes of Britain's historic town and city centres were cleared – where bomb damage had occurred but also in areas where no bombs had fallen. They were swept away for being old, as society looked to the future that they had been fighting for with great expectations. This impetus caused many architects and urbanists to feel that utopia was within sight.

Back-to-back terraced workers' housing, much of it built quickly and cheaply in the Victorian period, covered much of Britain's urban environment in the post-war period. Considered unsanitary and unsuitable, swathes of this type of housing stock were pulled down after the war. (Getty Images)

Did you know?

In 1956 the Smithsons showcased their 'House of the Future' at the Ideal Home Exhibition. Their progressive vision for the modern home was to create a curving structure of moulded plastic, with a stylish interior featuring futuristic furniture and a range of gadgets like electric bed-sheets, loud-speaker telephones and a sunken bathtub that rinses itself with detergent.

Post-war Britain was more receptive to modernism, albeit a softer, more Scandinavian version than the pure white boxes of the 1920s and '30s. This more domestic and less threatening second-generation modernism came to be known in the UK as Festival of Britain style, named for the festival which took place in 1951 and included, alongside wide-ranging architectural and art commissions for its South Bank location, a 'living architecture' exhibition: a rebuilt neighbourhood in Poplar, East London, called the Lansbury estate. The style employed at the Lansbury was the sanctified style for post-war rebuilding: clean, unfussy, of traditional material and form. This Festival style can be seen all over the country, at new towns like Harlow and rebuilding projects like central Coventry, as well as fitted into any other town you can mention. Modernism had found its popular British form, via Scandinavia.

This lonely remnant is the original boiler house of the Brynmawr rubber factory in South Wales, which used ground-breaking technologies and materials for British industrial design and is said to have inspired construction of the Sydney Opera House.

The Brynmawr rubber factory was a seminal building in the post-war landscape of British architecture. It was designed between 1946 and 1951 by the Architect's Co-op, collaborating with the engineer Ove Arup. Exploiting new materials and technologies, the building featured concrete barrel vaulting and sinuous, sculptural, functional forms that would become common in mid to late twentieth-century architecture. The building was widely celebrated at the time for its vision, conception and sophistication – it was hailed as a British modernist icon. It was the first post-war building to receive listed status in England and Wales, gaining Grade II* listing in 1985. Sadly, this didn't stop this important building being demolished in 2001. Only the two-storey boiler house with its inverted parabolic reinforced-concrete shell roof survives. Far more inventive and responsive than the early buildings of the style, Brynmawr showed Britain that modernism was on the move.

Le Corbusier also developed his post-war style away from the shocking simplicity of first-generation modernism to a more idiosyncratic and developed architectural language. Corb's apartment building the Unité d'habitation in Marseilles was seminal, as a concept and in its aesthetic, and its ideas went on to influence generations of architects. Originally designed in 1945 but taking five years to complete, this building was an architectural revolution. The structure's vast form together with its carefully balanced off-set of rectilinear and highly sculptural concrete, the dense massing, the enlivened facade with colourful contrasting panels, the vast elephantine legs that raise it up off the ground, the expression of the materials – structural concrete elevated to an art form – these things were all revolutionary. Here was a building that lived up to the epithet brutalism, although the term was not yet in use when the building was designed. The ultimate 'machine for living in' included shops, medical and educational facilities, playgrounds and a rooftop running track, all within a parkland setting. The design

Le Corbusier's epic Unité d'habitation in Marseille was an eighteen-storey slab block, completed in 1952. Five other Unités were built, including one in Berlin. (Getty Images)

embodied and encouraged the integration of healthy living, as well as the integration of art and life. Corb's later work, for example the chapel at Ronchamps of 1954, pushed concrete to even more exciting sculptural possibilities, emulating, even challenging nature in its unnatural forms.

Architects from across Europe flocked to see Corbusier's work for themselves, and came away buzzing with inspiration, with the confidence to go in bigger and bolder directions, to use heavier massing, to use sculptural forms, to create contradictory or confrontational buildings. These ideas, promulgated by British architects, helped to define mid-century architecture.

The term New Brutalism, as it first appeared, has been claimed as deriving from a number of sources. It seems that 'nybrutalism' was first used in Sweden by architect Hans Asplund in 1949 in reference to a house built by two of his contemporaries, who chose an industrial brick finish for an otherwise fairly unremarkable building. The powerful, plausible and frankly pleasurable phrase was picked up by visiting English architects and was soon to be heard in the UK although its meaning, translated into architecture, at this time is fairly vague. It was the Smithsons who took the phrase and ran with it (and at some time claiming credit for having invented it). Their adoption of the phrase was cemented and popularised by architectural critic Reyner Banham, who published an essay entitled 'The New Brutalism, ethics or aesthetics?' in 1955.

Did you know?

'The New Brutalism has to be seen against a background of the recent history of history, and, in particular, the growing sense of the inner history of the modern movement itself.'

Reyner Banham, 1955

The phrase claims homage to, and is regularly attributed as being directly derived from, the French phrase *béton brut*, meaning raw concrete. This Corbusian term relates to the use of raw materials – particularly exposed concrete finishes. It chimes with the honesty to materials and structural expression inherent in modernism. Banham also allies the term brutalism to Art Brut, a fairly obscure avant-garde Parisian art movement concerned with a particular style of naive art. These references afford the style associated intellectualism, but still don't describe the architecture beyond the basic qualities of modernism.

Concurrent with the theoretical background that fostered brutalism, a number of other more practical influencing factors came together in the 1950s and '60s that helped the popularisation of many of the movement's common themes. An expanding welfare state combined with a boom in cheap energy meant a significant amount of building was taking place or planned across Britain. When post-war material shortages were finally over in 1954, British local authorities, emboldened by planning reform, began proactively designing for the future. The rise of domestic car ownership sanctioned huge changes to our landscape, with the creation of new roads, motorways, car parks and so on. The new welfare state needed buildings. New housing should reflect shifts in social hierarchies, and integrate advanced technologies and labour-saving devices into our homes. Everyone should benefit from a decent home, warmed by clean and efficient central heating. Everyone could expect medical care, and free education for their children.

Rapid population growth meant a school building programme, followed by a university expansion programme. New civic buildings – town halls, law courts, libraries, theatres and cultural centres, as well as the more functional car parks and ring roads that served them – needed a new language of architecture fit for the future. Brutalism stepped in to respond to the major social and political issues of the post-war era. Brace yourself, Britain: brutalism is coming!

Sir Hugh Casson's design for an Elephant House at London Zoo, 1962–65, uses thick concrete on its external elevations, recollecting the tough hides of the elephants within. Windowless, gently curved, robust and strong, this building has much in common with brutalist architecture. (Getty Images)

3
Defining Characteristics

Understanding what brutalism isn't is key to understanding what brutalism is. The name here is particularly misleading. Architectural brutality could derive from ugliness, from sheer volume or from a building's sense of disharmony with its setting. While some may attribute these qualities to brutalist buildings, none of these things can be called defining characteristics of brutalism. There are two elements which all brutalist buildings share: firstly a particular honest expression of function, materials and services, and secondly, a certain mood.

The honest expression of materials and services (the *béton brut*) was first used as an architectural technique in the early twentieth century, but has subsequently gone on to feature in other buildings and architectural styles beyond brutalism. This alone, although important, cannot be used to define brutalist buildings. The single most important factor that defines a building or structure as truly brutalist is the most difficult to actually pin down – it is the building's mood.

Brutalist buildings have presence, they have drama. They don't have to be big, necessarily, but they have to be bold, to intimidate – to live up to their billing; to brutalise. As Reyner Banham wrote, the key characteristic is the building's 'bloody-mindedness'.

Thick, robust and hefty – brutalism replaced the delicate columns of earlier modernism with engorged legs to bring a greater sense of solidity to their buildings. Illustrated here is the Faculty of Modern and Medieval Languages, Cambridge.

The Denys Wilkinson building of 1967, designed by Philip Dowson of ARUP engineering. It houses the Oxford University Department of Physics. Nikolaus Pevsner said that this building marked 'the arrival of New Brutalism in Oxford'.

A brutalist building's massing and weight is central to this. Whereas first-generation modernism would be made up of finely balanced compositions, harmonised elements with volumes elevated on skinny piloti, brutalist buildings tend to be thunderously heavy, appearing to defy balance, to defy nature itself; brutalism introduced top-heavy elements and replaced the delicate piloti of the previous generation with engorged, monstrous columns, affording the buildings a much greater sense of weight and mass.

It is difficult to imagine now, but this type of architectural disharmony had never been seen before. Advancements in structural and reinforced concrete enabled buildings to grow, and their shapes and volumes to distort, emulating the natural world in sweeping curves and top-heavy forms. In twentieth-century architecture, curving shapes are often provided as counterpoint to rectilinear volumes, or massed repetitive elements. An example of this is the sculptural roof forms that provide relief to the scale and dense elevational treatment of the Unité d'habitation. The emulation of natural form in concrete is also a defiance of nature; never before had it been possible for these shapes to be replicated so confidently, and in such a massive, bloody-minded way. Rather than an architecture that aspires to blend comfortably into pastoral scenes, or strives for beauty through surface decoration like an ornamented object, brutalist buildings seem to aspire to recreate the sense of being surrounded by enclosing cliffs in some sort of nightmare, or the intense emotion of a thunderstorm. They take nature's more threatening elements and subvert them, encapsulating the whole in sculptural concrete.

Did you know?

Not all concrete buildings are brutalist, and not all brutalist buildings are concrete!

A common understanding is that the title brutalism derives solely from the phrase *béton brut*, and therefore that raw concrete buildings only are brutalist. This is not the case. The emphasis should be on the rawness, rather than the concrete. The 'raw' or 'honest' use of other materials can also produce brutalist buildings that are not principally constructed of, or otherwise characterised by, concrete.

Architecture before the twentieth century had relied on constructing a load-bearing structure and then largely covering this with a 'skin' of brick or stone. Often, cheaper materials inside

Park Hill, Sheffield. The repetition of the concrete frame is softened by the colour-graded choice of bricks to infill. Streets in the sky further articulate the elevations by providing the horizontal expression of balconies at every third floor. (Simon Reading)

were covered by a more expensive finish, while at the same time, services were concealed between the layers of the building. In brutalist buildings, the structural frame is generally left exposed as the finish; the honest expression of the structure and the materials. At Park Hill in Sheffield, Jack Lynn and Ivor Smith used an exposed structural concrete frame and in-filled the panels with brickwork. Collaborating with the artist John Forrester, four colours of brick were selected (purple, terracotta, red and cream), which were laid in a colour-graded way from darkest to lightest. Another outcome of eliminating the building's decorative 'skin' is that there is nowhere to hide the services. Brutalists apply the same sense of honesty to this, exposing, expressing, even celebrating the services. This is seen at the Smithsons' Hunstanton School, although the classic and most celebrated example is probably Erno Goldfinger's pair of housing estates in east and west London, the Brownfield and Cheltenham estates, more commonly known by the names of the respective towers, the Balfron Tower and the Trellick Tower.

Stirling and Gowan's building for the University of Leicester's engineering department (1958–63) does use structural concrete for its frame, and does use exposed concrete finishes internally with great success, but the characterising material of the building is red brick. The building plays the same tricks with weight and mass, defying gravity to cantilever a great sense of weight indelicately. This building rears up with confidence, suspending not only brick and glass, but disbelief. The obliquely located entrance draws you in beneath a disconcerting sense of the weight of the building above and around you. Approaching underneath the building's volume in this way heightens the drama. Further tricks are played using glass, ceramic tile and concrete to make sections of the building float or soar, or to make them feel heavy and burdensome as they balance above you. Even the more delicate element, the pyramidal glazing system of the workshop roofs, is strikingly spiky and robust. These seem out of reach as you approach, their serried ranks cleverly hidden, only hinted at by the end-pieces – indicating that they continue behind, above, beyond.

Above left: The engineering building at the University of Leicester by James Stirling. Industrial volumes of red brick are finely balanced against a modern glazing system to create a brutalist building of great tension.
Above right: James Stirling, 1926–92. Stirling worked in partnership with James Gowan from 1956 to 1963, then with Michael Wilford from 1971 until 1992. (Getty Images)
Below: Three-dimensional diamond rooflights make up the roof of the workshops at the Leicester engineering building.

The Cambridge History Faculty by James Stirling. Over-sailing wings provide a counter-balance to the cascading central section, wrapped around at lower level.

James Stirling designed a handful of buildings in this red-brick brutalist manner, including the Florey Building in Oxford, and the History Faculty in Cambridge. While exposed concrete is not the finish here either, the buildings' mood and massing still make them recognised brutalist masterpieces, and there remains an honesty to material; red brick invoking industrial heritage, large glazing systems bringing them bang up to date and engineering solutions subverting the parameters of predetermined architectural norms.

With this freedom of new materials, particularly of reinforced concrete, suddenly finishes became of major importance. When used industrially, little importance was attached to the material finish, but translated to a housing project or cultural centre, of course the finish had to be treated as artwork. The 'as found' ethic and aesthetic of brutalism influenced the finished appearance of the concrete.

Concrete in its simplest form is made up of a hydraulic binder such as Portland cement combined with aggregates and sand, mixed with water, then poured into moulds or shuttering and allowed to cure and set. Concrete can be poured in-situ, or can be pre-cast off site and transported. The properties of the finished material can be influenced by the selection of the components: from small to large aggregates (gravel, crushed stone, through to fine sand or silt), the range of sand from fine to course, and the methods of batching, compacting, mixing, even transporting, can give different effects to the finished appearance. The material can then be finished in a variety of ways; the mould or shuttering marks can be left exposed, honestly expressing the construction – a favourite brutalist hallmark. As shuttering is commonly formed of planks of wood, this will leave the impression of timber grain and plank marks in the concrete, creating a rich, warm and familiar texture. Alternatively, the formwork

Above: Ribbed and textured concrete details, Coventry. The ribbed finish on the left is achieved by inserting shaped formwork against which the poured concrete is allowed to set, leaving the rich indentation. Notice how the ribbed section has weathered differently, leaving coloured streaks on the surface.

Below left: Aggregate rich concrete. The finish here has been achieved by altering the mix of the concrete to include fine pebbles, affording a dense texture and natural feeling to this shuttered finish.

Below right: Board-marked concrete. The timber texture from the shuttering has indented the granular texture of wooden boards on the finished material, breaking down the appearance of the concrete to imply timber. Notice the shutter-release mark on the right.

This interior wall at the Barbican centre shows the textural effect of bush hammered concrete. This would have been hand-finished, and the depth of texture is revealed by the raking light.

could be faced with rubber, plastic or steel to create a variety of impressions – even ribbed to create deep indentations.

To achieve a finish that exposed the aggregate within the concrete, bush hammering would remove the smooth top layer of set concrete. (A bush hammer is a small stone chisel.) By selecting aggregate with particular qualities, for example shiny crushed quartz, you could ensure the qualities of the finished elevation. This gives concrete a huge versatility as a building material.

Rather than hiding the services that make the building work, as previous generations had done, now services are celebrated: the boiler house elevated as the pinnacle of the building, the shiny pipework or ventilation shafts celebrated, proudly and artistically displayed. At the Balfron and Trellick towers, architect Erno Goldfinger separates out the lift shaft and communal heating system, detaching them from the main body of the building, only connecting them via bridged walkways on every third floor. In part this was a practical arrangement to keep the noisy lifts away from the bedrooms of the flats, but it served also to highlight and venerate these new mechanical utilities, transforming them into design elements – showing how much better this bold, new style of high-rise housing was than its Victorian terraced predecessors; celebrating the technological advancement integral to this new breed of buildings – advancements that the lucky residents had never had before – and simultaneously creating a striking silhouette, affording the building a strongly recognisable identity.

Above left: Trellick Tower. The top-heavy left-hand service tower contains lifts, boiler housing and services, and is connected to the main block every three floors. The resultant silhouette made the building look tall, slender and achingly modern when it was designed.

Above right: Erno Goldfinger and his wife moved into a three bedroom flat at the Balfron Tower when it was completed in 1968. Their aim was to discover the advantages and disadvantages of life in a high-rise property. The findings of this exercise helped to shape the design for his second great tower, the Trellick. (Getty Images)

The facade treatment of both the Balfron and Trellick towers show clear links back to the Unité d'habitation. These regularly irregular patterns, where individual elements combine to form a whole sculptural elevation, can also be seen at Sheffield's Park Hill and the Smithsons' Robin Hood Gardens in London.

Did you know?

Hungarian-born architect Erno Goldfinger (1902–87) had an influence beyond his buildings. The writer Ian Fleming reputedly heard the name Goldfinger from a cousin of the architect's wife, and 'borrowed' it for use as that of a Bond villain! Needless to say the architect was not impressed, and although he threatened to take legal action, it seems he eventually learnt to live with it.

Architecture and construction have always been distinguishable. Architecture has a theory behind it – it has aspiration. Construction is the result of needing to erect a building or structure in the most cost-effective way. In the later twentieth century, architecture and construction diverged more than ever before. Cost became the driver of so much building work. Many buildings from the same period of brutalism – and buildings that

Elevational detail of a car park in Northampton. While form is following function here, and the structural concrete provides the finish, the structure lacks the menacing mood or bloody-minded spirit that would make it a recognised brutal building.

have come since – look the way they do because this is a cheap and cost-effective way to build. Exposed concrete became a normal material; expressed structural elements were not always a revolutionary statement driven by idealist theory – they were often simply a solution to drive down costs. Sanctioned in a way by brutalism, cheap, often fairly ugly concrete structures began to appear across the British landscape. Ironically enough, the word brutal is a fairly good word for this type of building. In any town or city you will find brash, mid and late twentieth-century buildings, built using pre-cast elements and concrete frames. They loom, they brutalise their landscape even; but these buildings would not be described as brutalism.

Once you begin to appreciate the difference, this fascinating subject comes alive. Brutalist buildings are more distinguished, refined. They are poetic and appear to encapsulate movement, the intersection of the forms becoming dynamic. Johann Wolfgang von Goethe, a German writer and statesman (1749–1832), described architecture as 'frozen music', and the soaring volumes of brutalism prove that comparison true. Jack Lynn, one of the architects of Park Hill in Sheffield, compared their design to 'a bloody great fugue, all the parts are little themes with little bits of tunes and variations that spread'.

The analogy of a fugue is a good one. Brutalist buildings use repeated details and techniques on a small scale which come together on a much larger scale, marshalled into a symphony, or cacophony, depending on your view.

Like many architects of the period, Denys Lasdun did not consider himself a brutalist. He disliked and rejected the term, and felt that his buildings were driven more by humanism

The South Bank home of the National Theatre by Denys Lasdun, seen here under construction in January 1975. This building has the honourable distinction of having featured in both the top ten 'most loved' and top ten 'most hated' London buildings simultaneously in opinion polls. (Getty Images)

Sir Denys Lasdun, 1914–2001. One of the most eminent of British architects in the twentieth century. He was awarded the RIBA gold medal in 1977. (Getty Images)

than brutalism. While his recognised masterpiece, the National Gallery on London's South Bank, is generally considered to be brutal in its dynamic intersecting forms, over-sailing mass and concrete finishes, Lasdun took great pains to ensure the shuttering brought out the grain and texture of the wooden planks in order to soften the harsh material, and to root the building in the vernacular language of traditional British timber architecture. He even insisted that each shuttering plank be used only twice, once on either side, so as not to erode the qualities of the wood grain through over-use. Externally, weathering has diminished this subtle textural finish, but internally Lasdun's intentions were clear, and the rich texture of the columns and walls can be read as the architect intended.

The style is not the first time in architecture that this sense of drama has been created. Brutalism owes a lot to, and replicates significant elements of both the Victorian gothic and the baroque. All three movements subverted, created drama and aimed to break the rules and suspend disbelief. It is interesting that many people assume brutalist architects were rejecting architectural history; in fact brutalism owes a lot to classical architectural forms, massing and layout.

Nicholas Hawksmoor's London churches of the early eighteenth century used the prescribed elements of classical architecture, but applied them without the rules. The Victorians' modern gothic loomed, glowered and intimidated, drawing on medieval design templates but applying modern technologies to create an architecture of the monstrous. And so in the twentieth century, in reaction to the twee, soft Scandinavian modernism that looked to become de-rigeur, brutalism performed the same tricks, subverting, over-sailing and exploiting modern technologies to dramatic effect. Furthered by the title brutalism and all the connotations that go with it, and while hailed as misunderstood masterpieces by some, they were considered concrete monstrosities by many. Right from the start they divided opinion but this did not stop their unavoidable explosion across the British landscape.

Olivier Theatre

Dorfman Theatre

The dynamic shapes and balance of light and dark is here revealed inside the National Theatre, South Bank, London. The delicacy of approach to the shuttering can be best appreciated inside, where weathering has not eroded the finish. (Used with the Kind permission of the National Theatre)

4

An Explosion of British Brutalism: Housing and Culture

In the late 1950s the Smithsons had declared themselves the 'new brutalists'. Having adopted this catchy slogan, what were they going to do with it?

The first building launched upon the world by these self-proclaimed new brutalists was a secondary school in Hunstanton, Norfolk (1949–54). This had actually been designed some years earlier, but by the time of its completion, it was really all anyone had to attribute to brutalism. The building's form and composition don't really live up to their brutal billing – fairly sedate long, low rectilinear blocks emulate Mies Van der Rohe and the proportions of Palladian classicism. But the choice of materials and the manner of honestly expressing those materials, as well as the structure and services, is where the roots of brutalism can be seen.

From modest, theoretical ideas and an experimental school building in Norfolk, brutalism went on to epitomise mid to late twentieth-century urban architecture in Britain, be that a good or bad thing. The next two chapters will look at a small selection of brutalist buildings of Britain, grouped in common themes of residential, civic buildings, transport architecture and university expansion.

Housing

The growing requirements for residential buildings in the mid-twentieth century would only be met by exploiting modern materials and technologies, and, critically, by building upwards. Scale and ease of mass production, and the expense spared in eschewing decorative materials and finishes, meant that brutalism naturally lent itself to fill this gap.

The City of London was appointing architects around this time to re-plan and rebuild large areas of bomb damage. A competition for a housing estate at Golden Lane was held in the early 1950s and the winning submission was by a lecturer of architecture at Kingston Polytechnic called Geoffrey Powell, who, upon securing the commission, formed a practice with two colleagues, creating the firm Chamberlin, Powell & Bon. This first commission

The use of industrial materials such as the steel columns, and regular, modular repeating forms made the Hunstanton School by Peter and Alison Smithson a revolutionary building for its time. (Bob Giddings)

Service tower (and later bike sheds) at Hunstanton School. Separating and celebrating services, rather than concealing them, was a new concept in architecture, and went on to characterise brutalism. (Bob Giddings)

Two of the residential towers at the Barbican estate. The gentle curve of Frobisher crescent can just be seen between them. These were the tallest residential towers in London when built, at 123 metres (404 ft). (Sylvia Warman)

Architects Peter Chamberlin, Geoffry Powell and Christoph Bon at the Guildhall, London, in 1956, discussing a model of their proposed development at the Barbican estate in the City of London. (Getty Images)

led to a later, much more significant commission from the City of London, which would ultimately become the Barbican estate.

Did you know?

Poster-boy for British brutalism, the Barbican estate covers a 35-acre site and is constructed of over 130,000 cubic metres of concrete. On opening the complex, Queen Elizabeth II described it as 'one of the modern wonders of the world'.

With three tall residential towers and numerous lower level groups of terraces and buildings forming a range of intimate spaces, the Barbican also included formal and semi-formal gardens, an arts centre with theatre and cinema, public library, a dentist, pubs and even a fire station – the whole raised above ground level services and car parking. The Barbican is a village within a city, with its own confident, chunky and rough-hewn aesthetic. While turning its back on the traditional buildings and urban grain of the area, it also integrates sections of Roman wall and a medieval church, which are offset by the dynamic architecture like treasured historical objects. Massed repetitive elements are consciously softened by repeated curved forms at roof level, by a cunningly located crescent, and furthermore by planting, playful water features and careful management of views. The whole place has an undeniable solidity, derived from its scale – true on both the macro and micro level. The variety of pick hammered, bush hammered and brush hammered finishes of the concrete is exceptional.

The Smithsons' Robin Hood Gardens in Tower Hamlets also used a massive scale, with a Corbusian repeating facade treatment to break this down. They piled the flats high to allow a parkland setting between the two blocks, and used the massing to shield the parkland from the heavily trafficked road behind, bestowing their snaking blocks with a confident muscularity. Similarly to Goldfinger, the Smithsons separate to celebrate the technology, lift and boiler housing.

Above: Playful water features and soft planting both reinforce and soften the chunky concrete aesthetic of the Barbican, City of London.

Below left: The name Barbican comes from a defensive tower, part of the Roman city wall that traversed the site. Chamberlin, Powell & Bon took the ideas and motifs of a fortress and incorporated them into their designs.

Below right: Elevational detail of Robin Hood Gardens, East London, prior to demolition. The rigidity of the concrete grid that formed the elevations was softened by variation in repetition. Services are contained at the end of the block.

Left: Keeling House, Tower Hamlets, London. Lasdun designed the building as a reinvention of the traditional terraced housing it was to replace. The only variation in the elevational treatment is the fifth floor, where single-storey old people's flats represented the maximum height a fire-fighter's ladder could reach.
Below: Internal detail from Lasdun's Keeling House. The 'spaces in-between' offer interesting views and provide entrance balconies and services to the flats.

Denys Lasdun's Keeling House, also in Tower Hamlets, is quite different. A single tall block in a relatively low-rise neighbourhood, Lasdun intended to reinvent the traditional terraced housing by stacking a series of maisonettes atop each other, with principal rooms facing outwards to maximise views. The block is formed of three intersecting chunks of tower, seemingly frozen in an elaborate dance, having clustered together but being still quite separate. The shared entrance balconies create opportunities for neighbours to meet and chat, and the intersecting elements of the building create interesting angles which offer snatches of view through, up, down and outwards. The three sections of the building seem to hover around their core, which houses lifts, stairs and services.

The utilisation of unique spaces and incidentally generated views are similar to those hidden spaces used for residential access at the Brunswick Centre, 1967–72, by Patrick Hodgkinson – a complex mega-structure consisting of two A-framed blocks linked by a raised podium containing shops and services. The whole group sits in among the restrained Georgian squares of Bloomsbury in Central London. Each one of over 500 flats is light and airy and includes a balcony. They are accessed from the central, hollowed out space within the A-frame, which exploits the dramatic vertical views as well as enabling the supply of services. This 'machine for living' was designed so that it could be continually extended – the architect's vision was that later phases would eventually reach all the way north to the Euston Road.

Concrete is used in similar forms at the Alexandra and Ainsworth estate in Camden. Designed by Neave Brown for the Camden Architect's Department in 1968 and built 1972–78, this project reinterprets the traditional street, and its form focuses the lives of its residents away from the noisy main-line railway north of the site, where car parking and services are provided, towards the more convivial pedestrianised central street, with cascading planted balconies softening the scale and the toughness of the concrete.

Another infamous mega-structure is the Park Hill estate in Sheffield city centre, opened in 1961. Jack Lynn and Ivor Smith's complex design follows the natural topography of the site, so while it rises from four to thirteen storeys, it maintains a level roof line, and every access level has direct access from the ground. These open-air decks provide 'streets in the sky' (another Corbusian concept), 3-metre wide communal walkways wide enough for neighbours to meet and interact, for children to play, even for a milk float to drive around.

Industrial looking stacks demark the cut-away entrances in this mega-housing estate, the Brunswick Centre, Bloomsbury, London, by Patrick Hodgkinson. The recessing balconies provide generous light as well as outdoor space to all of the flats.

Above: Also known as Rowley Way, the Alexandra and Ainsworth estate in Camden, North West London, is constructed from in-situ board-marked unpainted reinforced concrete. (Getty Images)

Left: Every third floor at Park Hill in Sheffield was provided with an access deck. These balconies (streets in the sky) articulate the façade but also provide entrances to flats, and social spaces for residents. (Simon Reading)

Civic buildings

The Birmingham Central Library, completed in 1974 by John Madin, now demolished, was certainly confident enough to have been described as bloody-minded. Its seemingly windowless bulk rose and stepped outwards in an inverted ziggurat – distinctive amidst the grand, traditional Victorian civic buildings of central Birmingham – although the library's height was restricted in order that it remained subservient to its neighbours. Good, well-behaved, classical buildings diminish as they rise. The bold geometry of Madin's library took exactly the opposite approach. The library was intended as part of a wider civic masterplan for Birmingham which was never fully executed. The slashed budget for the library instead meant the finishes were never of as high a quality as originally intended. The raw structural concrete continued onto the inside with coffered concrete ceilings and ribbed concrete walls showing exposed aggregate. Again, the visitor was required to approach underneath the building's looming weight, through into a light-filled entrance lobby with glass curtain walling revealing views of the Victorian town hall. The visitor's journey continued from low, dark spaces into double-height, light-filled spaces – the 'light' (or knowledge) inside gradually being revealed.

For a time the largest non-national library in Europe, Birmingham Central Library opened in 1974 and closed in 2013. It was demolished in 2016. The internal walls were of ribbed concrete with locally sourced round aggregate exposed by abrasive blasting. (Getty Images)

The curved wing to the right of this picture formed the lending library. The reference library was housed in the eight-storey square block to the left, designed around an open atrium above a public square. (Getty Images)

A detail of the sculptural form and shuttered concrete finish of the Tricorn Centre, Portsmouth, 1966–2004. The site once housed the largest Laser Quest arena in Europe. (Getty Images)

In Portsmouth, following substantial war damage, a whole new town centre was planned and executed with confidence. The centrepiece for this was the Tricorn Centre of 1966, which encompassed shops, a nightclub, two pubs, eight flats and a huge car park for 400 cars, expressed in a brutalist manner by the Owen Luder Partnership under the direction of Rodney Gordon. Corbusian ideas are used here time and time again. Sadly, the big name stores never moved in, and the centre always suffered for it, quickly filling up with discount stores – the brutal architecture providing an easy scapegoat for the failings of the site. Instead of being cleaned up, revived and celebrated, it was pulled down in 2004.

Did you know?

Despite being demolished in 2004, Portsmouth's Tricorn Centre still continues to win awards for its architecture. In 2009 a group of architects calling themselves 'the Rubble Club' awarded the Tricorn the 'best demolished building' award at a ceremony in Nottingham.

Denys Lasdun built a number of important buildings across the country. The Royal College of Physicians (Regent's Park) demonstrates how his work is often retrospectively defined as brutalist, despite his rejection of the phrase. Lasdun's National Theatre complex on London's South Bank is perhaps one of the best known and most high-profile sites now considered part of the canon of brutalism. The composition, detail and finish are exceptional here. The visitor is drawn in underneath top-heavy blocks to dark entrances which subsequently open up to reveal a captivating series of spaces. The building revels in the most surprising glimpsed and framed views, balancing and counterbalancing, juxtaposing and contradicting itself with simple complexity. While the building is initially disorientating, it is actually masterfully guiding the visitor through a very simple series of spaces, directing you to exciting views, moving you from darkness to light and back again.

Right: The Royal College of Physicians, London, by Denys Lasdun. The overhanging, rectilinear forms contrast with the formal classical setting of Nash's Regent's Park terraces.

Below: Royal College of Physicians. In the foreground is the part-submerged lecture hall, using an industrial brick finish and complex curving form to counterbalance the more strict geometry of the main building behind.

The National Theatre on London's South Bank. Strong horizontal and vertical planes and careful cut-aways offset each other to combine into a masterful design.

This double external staircase at the National Theatre invites the visitor into the dark space underneath this finely balanced volume, which brings you up to the terrace level and rewards you with fantastic views across the River Thames.

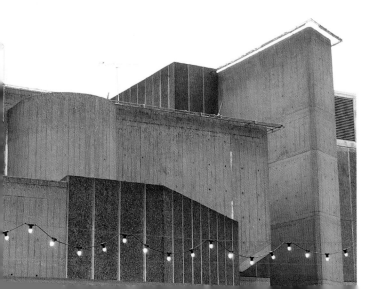

Detail of the Southbank Centre, London. The varying volumes, spaces and services are expressed differently in concrete, initially disorientating but on further study they coalesce into an impressive brutalist landscape.

The wider South Bank Centre wraps around the National Theatre and includes the Hayward Gallery, Queen Elizabeth Hall and Purcell Rooms – opened in 1968, conceived as additions to the existing Southbank arts complex and designed by the Greater London Council Architect's Department. The complex inter-relation of these building elements, together with large external decks (intended for outdoor displays of public sculpture), circulation via walkways and exterior staircases, separated service roads and car parking, formal and informal spaces are initially confusing and can be disorientating. In fact they are in a fairly complex way responding to the site, and are rich and generous in the spaces and views that they gift to the public realm. This is one of the world's foremost places of public perambulation, a place to go just to walk around and enjoy – an increasing rarity in urban centres, and all the more precious for it. The concrete forms and the range of spaces generated inside and out facilitate and integrate art and life. Adaptation over time has changed the way the public move around the site, sometimes not for the better – but some unexpected and unintended uses, such as the skateboarding undercroft, have developed organically and achieved international fame.

The Queen Elizabeth Hall and the Purcell Room, Southbank Centre, London. Rainwater running down the overhanging form of the building has caused sooty staining of the concrete beneath. Is this merely dirt, an indicator that the building requires intensive maintenance, or is it simply the patina of history?

The Skaters' Undercroft at the Southbank Centre was not an intended use, but has become internationally significant to the skateboarding community, who successfully campaigned to save the space from commercial redevelopment.

5
An Explosion of British Brutalism: Transport and Education

As concrete and the freedom it allowed designers flourished, it was used extensively in transportation and infrastructure, but commonly in construction rather than architecture. The underpass or ring road may brutalise their landscape, but brutalist they are not; the intention of the designers was not to subvert the status quo, or to intimidate or delight through sculptural forms – rather it was to get the job done economically. There are, however, a handful of moments when transport infrastructure and brutalism do come together, which are explored here.

Transport

The Preston bus station and car park by Keith Ingham and Charles Wilson of architectural firm BDP is a brutalist icon. Its massed repetitive elements combined with its scale afford it undertones of science fiction. This building truly anticipates the machine age future, integrating passengers and modern transportation. Its qualities of pattern and the repetitious

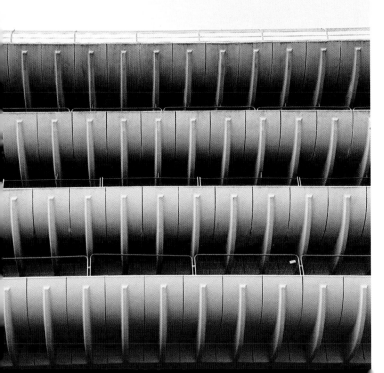

Recently cleaned fins, comprising the swept-up edge of each deck of the multi-storey car park above Preston bus station. The regular repetition of solid and void here expresses the industrialism of the architecture.
(Andrea Perrot)

Deep coffers within the pre-formed concrete ceiling bring an industrial feel to the interior of the Preston bus station. The simple volume is efficient and legible, aiding the building's users. (Andrea Perrot)

light concrete set against dark shadow give both dramatic contrast and an instantly recognisable form. The curving pre-cast sculptural fins and sweeping access ramps detach the building from traditional architecture, ushering in a machine age future and elevating something functional to something beautiful.

The Trident car park in Gateshead, sadly demolished but immortalised in the film *Get Carter* (and subsequently known as the '*Get Carter* car park') was designed in 1962 by the Owen Luder Partnership, with the linked shopping centre being completed in 1969. Similar to Preston, it stood out from its surroundings, expressing function clearly in its form. The stripped back staircases are a motif that this building shared with many other brutal buildings – a practical way of paring down a necessary element into an essential, sculptural form. Brutal to its bones, the car park is clearly related to the Portsmouth Tricorn Centre. The inclusion of a roof-top nightclub was an inspired design move, but sadly a lease was never agreed. Finally, the whole thing was demolished in 2010.

The freedom of new materials was employed expressively and brutally at the Birstall petrol station in Leicester, commissioned from 1966 and executed in the late 1960s. Designed by Eliot Noyes for the US-based Mobil Oil Corporation, the structure employs six intersecting mushroom-like canopies made up of steel posts and canopy frames. Many of these designs were built across the world but few survive. The example at Leicester has been heavily over-clad and re-branded, and the original cylindrical pumps replaced, but the super-structure remains and is Grade II listed.

Above: The dynamic forms of the *Get Carter* car park, Gateshead, during demolition. 34,000 tonnes of concrete were used in its construction. (Getty Images)

Below: The intersecting mushroom canopies that form the Birstall Garage in Leicester. The structure has been altered and over-clad, but the exciting forms of the 1960s remain legible.

The Forton Services restaurant tower of 1965 by T. P. Bennet. Located on the M6 in Lancashire, this was cutting edge architecture in its day, and recalls the glamour and optimism of the 1960s transport revolution.

The northbound M6 motorway in Lancashire is home to a striking piece of brutalism – the Forton Services restaurant tower. Designed to capture all the mid-1960s glamour of international air travel, this motorway service structure looks like an air traffic control tower, but in fact housed a restaurant catering to hungry motorway drivers topped by an optimistic 'sun deck'. Designed together with the low-level buildings and a pedestrian bridge-link by architectural firm T. P. Bennet in 1965, the hexagonal design of the elevated restaurant was carried through the complex. Even original staircases were hexagonal, and a pair of pentagonal lifts added a further futuristic touch. Sadly, the low-level buildings have been so heavily adapted that the original design is compromised. The hexagonal staircase has been removed, and the staircases leading to the restaurant and sun deck could not meet modern evacuation regulations, meaning the upper levels have been closed since 1989. The ambition and optimism of the 22-metre structure is still evident, even in dereliction.

The Apollo Pavilion is a 1969 structure, an art installation and also a bridge, designed for the new town of Peterlee, County Durham, in the late 1960s by artist Victor Pasmore. Featuring both fair-faced and bush hammered concrete, the structure consists of interlocking cubic volumes straddling the end of a small lake, and originally had abstract murals on the inward elevations. It was Pasmore's gift to the new town, where he had been involved in the design team. The structure was listed at Grade II* in 2011.

Did you know?

Restoration of the Apollo Pavilion featured repairs to areas of exposed aggregate, bush hammered and fair faced concrete, each requiring different methods. The most challenging element was finding a good match for the aggregate. The aggregate originally used was marine pebbles of mixed colours. After extensive research, materials for repairs were sourced from a beach in Hartlepool.

Left: Victor Pasmore's Apollo Bridge in Peterlee, County Durham, was named for the Apollo space programme, referencing the optimism of the time. Pasmore was the Consulting Director of Architectural Design of the Peterlee Development Corporation and conceived the bridge as a piece of architecture, art, sculpture and play equipment, as well as a means of crossing the lake. (Getty Images)

Below: The Birmingham Signal Box with its corrugated concrete exterior may polarise opinion, but it performs a vital function, housing arguably the city's most important infrastructure systems that serve one of the UK's busiest rail interchanges.

In Birmingham, a new railway signal box was designed in 1964 by architects Bicknell & Hamilton. This stand-out structure is composed of horizontal pre-cast sections of concrete cladding of a striking, spiky triangular profile on a reinforced concrete frame, punctuated by strongly emphasised horizontal metal-framed windows. Reminiscent of war-time bunkers, the design develops the functional form with strongly sculptural detailing, combining to make a highly distinctive, brutalist gem.

Above and below: At the time of its listing, English Heritage said of the Moore Street electricity substation: 'The scrupulously-finished concrete of the brutalist electricity substation on Moore Street in Sheffield, gives this bold building a dramatic, sculptural feel … It was an important component of the radical post-war regeneration of Sheffield, helping to revitalise the city after it was badly bombed.' (Simon Reading)

Perhaps more infrastructure than transport, the Moore Street electricity substation in Sheffield was designed in 1968 by Jefferson Sheard. The sub-station was described as a 'citadel' at the time of construction, and features sculptural wrap-around glazing to the external walkways, and a mixture of strongly expressed horizontals and verticals in pre-formed concrete, utilising shuttering on its over-sailing framework, aggregate-rich pre-cast panels and a strongly expressed stair tower. At parapet level, concrete coping panels flare outwards with gaps at the projecting roof beams, undulating in silhouette and glowering down upon passers-by, lending an ominous, strikingly brutalist quality.

Universities

A significant boom in university building created a wealth of commissions for architects across the country. The first wave became known as the 'Shakespeare Seven' so similar were their names to those retainers of Richard III in the famous play. This section introduces just some of the brutalist university buildings in Britain.

The University of East Anglia is perhaps the most notable, a campus university built on a new, out of town site from 1961 onwards, to designs by Denys Lasdun. The famous 'ziggurat' halls of residence were described by Lasdun as a series of architectural hills and valleys, an example of the architectural defiance of nature. As a result, the buildings themselves are the landscape, formed within a parkland setting. Although Lasdun designed the first buildings and master-planned the site, it was completed by other architects.

St Anne's College in Oxford commissioned the firm HKPA (Howell, Killick, Partridge & Amis) to design new accommodation for them in 1960. Completed by 1969, the Wolfson and Rayne buildings and linked blocks of college rooms sinuously wrapped around circular staircases. Undulation renders a fabulous interplay of solid and void, window and wall, punctuated by balconies. Pre-cast concrete panels stand out against board-marked, in situ cast concrete.

HKPA also designed the Hilde Besse Building at St Anthony's College, Oxford, in 1966. It was complete by 1971, when it scooped both a RIBA architecture award and a Concrete Society award. A reinterpretation of the traditional collegiate hall, this building uses pre-cast

Lasdun described the ziggurats of these halls of residence at the University of East Anglia as a series of architectural hills and valleys. (Getty Images)

William Howell, John Killick, John Partridge and Stanley Amis met in 1950 at the architect's department of the London County Council, where they designed the acclaimed Roehampton Lane estate (now known as Alton West, parts of which are listed at Grade II and II*).

projecting window bays above, strip windows below and a recessed, glazed ground floor to counter-balance the great weight of the structure. The projecting stair towers cleverly contrast heaviness and lightness, with substantive concrete panels offset by delicate vertical strip glazing to the corners. Internally, contrasting diagonals, exposed structural expression and finely balanced solid walls and framed views continue the masterful marriage of traditional form and layout with modern material and detailing.

The educational commission by HKPA that is perhaps most celebrated is the group of houses and flats for visiting mathematicians at Warwick University, of 1968–70. These are stripped-back brick buildings, with further exposed brickwork internally and cantilevered, concrete tread staircases – honest expressions of the materials, used in a robust, almost industrial way but resulting in a delicate and thoughtful composition. The curving brickwork allows continuous blackboard walls within the study spaces – form very much following function. The intricate plan comes together into a clear and strong design, expressing a highly considered approach to function and an extremely high quality use of materials.

At Leeds University, Chamberlin, Powell & Bon built the magnificent Roger Stevens Building, completed in 1970. The building's tense verticality is emphasised across the elevation by the muscular expression of cylindrical shafts (like organ pipes) and a staircase. Internal raked lecture theatres further inform the building's shape. Linking walkways and a reflecting pool tie the building into its landscape, making sense of the bold external forms.

The Cambridge History Faculty, built 1964–8, is the second of James Stirling's red-brick brutalist buildings. A reinforced concrete frame enables the striking form of this structure, finished in red brick and tile and patent glazing, affording dramatic views within as well as out of the faculty. It is generally considered to house the finest of Stirling's interiors. The design moves away from the imbalanced asymmetry of the Leicester Engineering Department

Above and left: The Hilde Besse Building at St Anthony's College, Oxford. An article from the time of its opening called HKPA's building '… beautifully detailed and a tour de force in articulation.' It went on to say that '… the lasting impression one retains from both the interior and exterior of the building is that of elegance and amenity.'

Above and below: Once considered futuristic enough for filming an episode of *Doctor Who*, the Roger Stevens building, with its striking 'organ pipe' elevational treatment, is an acclaimed design by Chamberlin, Powell & Bon that was originally part of a much larger, unexecuted masterplan for Leeds University. (Ali Boon)

Above: Mathematicians' houses, Warwick University. The group comprises five houses and two flats built using yellow Stourbridge bricks and with flat roofs. The houses are of two storeys and have single-storey extensions at the front and back. The front extension provides a porch and laundry room while the rear incorporates a study.

Left: Front elevation of the Matthew Building at the University of Dundee: a flat-roofed mega-structure of partially exposed pre-cast concrete frame and panel construction. The glass entrance canopy which forms a reception area was added in 2012.

towards a more symmetrical but still exhilarating form. The architects pushed the available technologies of the day to their limits to create a ground-breaking piece of architecture.

The Matthew Building of 1969–74 at the University of Dundee is a good example of a quiet yet confident piece of brutalism – a long sausage of a building that bumps its way down a sloping site, by Professor James Paul of Baxter, Clark & Paul. The main elevation is a section through the whole, and provides a legible yet playful frontage to the street, composed, yet not of an alien scale to neighbouring buildings. The side elevation, the building's long section, snakes back up the hillside, shape-shifting as it goes. The external elevations in concrete and glass are secondary; it is the series of internal spaces that generate them. The lecture halls, classrooms, workshops and corridors dictate the forms of the building; the solids, voids, the glazing coalesce into a convincing whole, with the services treated in the same manner, honestly expressed on both inside and out as their use predicts. Inside, large teaching spaces and more intimate conversation places weave together, creating a unified, brutalist narrative and a very practicable, working building.

Dunelm House by the Architects Co-Partnership and Arup engineers, built as a student centre at Durham University in 1966, is an astonishing building in an astonishing setting. The quirky design, encompassing a wide range of types of spaces opening up from a plunging central 'street', allows for wonderful views across the river and (some people think) appears wonderfully in views back, enjoying a particularly special relationship with the Kingsgate Bridge.

At St Andrews University in Fife, the Andrew Melville Hall by James Stirling was built in 1967 using prefabricated concrete modules. The patterned qualities of the concrete panels set alternatively create a rich herringbone texture. The large and unrelenting scale of the building as it snakes away down the hillside is therefore tempered on closer inspection by the surprising delicacy of the concrete finish. The structure follows the hillside, stepping down, and clearly expresses the form of the rooms within – repetitive cellular student rooms to the external elevations, the common rooms and kitchens expressed by glazing on the internal. Servicing clips in at the rear of the site.

These are just a small selection of brutalist buildings that are out there waiting to be explored. In addition to these categories, there are examples of many other brutalist building types across Britain, including private houses, industrial buildings, railway structures, and office and commercial buildings.

Andrew Melville Hall was constructed by industrialised process: pre-cast wall panels were craned into place. The buildings' geometry follows through to the irregular octagonal shape of the bedrooms. Errors in construction meant that extensive remedial work was required once it was complete, and because of this plans for further buildings at St Andrews to the same design were scrapped.

6
Loathe It

From the outset, brutal buildings have had a difficult time. Vocal resistance to their construction, and particularly to their 'brutality', was rife from the very beginning.

A turning point in the public imagination can be linked to the fateful 1968 Ronan Point disaster, in Canning Town, East London, in which five people died when a gas explosion blew out a load-bearing wall and caused the progressive collapse of a large section of the twenty-two-storey building. The pre-cast panel construction used a technique known as Large Panel System Building, essentially casting large, prefabricated concrete panels off-site and then bolting them together to erect the building. The tower was one of eight constructed in this way in Canning Town by the London Borough of Newham between 1965 and 1968. An inquiry found that the collapse was due to the poor quality construction, particularly an over-reliance on load-bearing joints. Major changes to UK building regulations followed this tragedy. It was fortunate that it occurred early in the morning while most residents were still asleep, or else many more would have died. While the block was not brutalist, it caused a shift in perception and a loss of public confidence around tall buildings and concrete construction; people began to believe that they were cheaply built and dangerous. Brutalist buildings, being of contemporary construction to Ronan Point and similarly characterised by concrete, suffered by association.

The novelty of the mega-housing estates did not last for long. With corners cut in specified materials, and budget-cutting to planned cyclical maintenance, these places soon revealed inherent flaws and started not only to look shabby, but to actually fall apart.

The defining characteristics of brutalism hammered home the dissatisfaction and became a rod to beat it with. The intimidating scale, the sense of drama – this often achieved by

Boarded up, fenced off and dangerous. Failed flats on the Brownfield estate, East London.

the contrast between small, dark spaces leading out into large, well-lit spaces – became the hallmarks of bad buildings. Confusing, even labyrinthine, dark spaces provided plenty of opportunity to lurk, loiter or leap out. The perceived threat of unseen assailants multiplied the fear, and the architecture was to blame. Dark corners lacking natural surveillance – whether in a car-park or a cultural centre – became, in the public consciousness at least, dangerous and the architecture came to represent the threat of violence. As people avoided these places, so they became wind-swept, transitory spaces, multiplying the fear. This was an architecture out of control. The architects of Park Hill even recognised that a lack of natural overlooking from windows onto their walkways was a mistake, as it led to a lack of ownership, a lack of community and the opportunity for anti-social behaviour. The intimidating architecture became so associated with social ills that they became inseparable, seen as both causing and reflecting each other.

Above right: Poorly specified concrete will spall (break off in fragments.) If water can get in behind the surface it can make the metal reinforcements rust. They will then expand, further cracking the concrete and leading to staining and further corrosion.
Below: An unrestored elevation declared a dangerous structure at Park Hill, Sheffield. The estate is being restored, but surely it should be pulled down instead? (Simon Reading)

Danger
Unsafe structure
urbansplash

Did you know?

Anthony Burgess's dystopian classic novel *A Clockwork Orange* was filmed on the Thamesmead estate, and purposefully exploited the brutalist architecture as a motif for intimidation, violence and a break-down of society.

While Corbusier's Unité d'habitation sparkled in the southern French sunshine, the colder climes of northern Europe did not present the buildings in the same light. Visit any British brutalist 'masterpiece' on a cold, grey, rainy day and you can struggle to appreciate its more admirable qualities. Concrete finishes spalled and stained in rain. If the mix was not quite right in the first place, the concrete would erode, exposing metal reinforcements, which would then rust, and streak and stain the façade. The curved, over-sailing decks of Preston bus garage quickly became stained with drips, creating a neglected and depressing appearance. Rusting reinforcements, crumbling concrete and rain-streaked surfaces do not lift the spirits.

If this was the brave new world, the younger generation in the 1970s and '80s were ready to react against it.

The seminal Hunstanton School may have looked wonderfully sleek, and may have been tremendously innovative with material and brave in design, but testimonies by those who used it regularly recount its impractical layout, problems with acoustics, heating, ventilation, windows, atmospheric control, condensation and more. What use is a beautiful building if it

Grimy concrete, vehicle ramps and graffiti-covered walls at the Thamesmead estate, where the bleak ambience and spiral of decline meant that what was once envisaged as a brave new world quickly ended up as a no-go area. (Getty Images)

A grey day in Preston. This oversized building and its scruffy surroundings could not be called a masterpiece, surely? (Andrea Perrot)

doesn't work for the activities it was designed for? The Pimlico School by John Bancroft for the GLC, built 1967–70 (and famously described as a 'battleship'), suffered similarly from bad user-reviews, although much admired by architectural historians. It was demolished in 2010 and replaced with an efficient new school building.

On 30 May 1984, Prince Charles made a speech at an event celebrating the 150th anniversary of the Royal Institute of British Architects (RIBA). He took the opportunity to lambast the state of modern architectural design, and decried a proposed (un-built) extension to the National Gallery by architect Peter Ahrends as like a 'monstrous carbuncle on the face of a much-loved and elegant friend'. This seminal 'monstrous carbuncle' speech has echoed through the intervening decades, dividing opinion. The response for those who concur with the Prince's views has been to embolden the denigration of the brash, bolshy brutalists in favour of a more comfortable, familiar architecture based on pastiches of historical styles. This is exemplified by Prince Charles's own development at Poundbury, an 'urban village' extension to Dorchester in Dorset, begun in 1993, where traditionalism is king in both street layout and the facade treatment of individual buildings.

The Prince did not make this comment in isolation. In a 1988 BBC documentary entitled *A Vision of Britain*, he famously said that John Madin's 1974 brutalist Birmingham Central Library looked like a 'place where books are incinerated, not kept'.

Prince Charles insists he did not intend to kickstart a battle of the styles; however, over the subsequent decades the debate in architecture has remained polarised, neatly summarised as a war between classicists and modernists. The word brutal fits neatly in with derogatory

Above: Exteriors of some of the notorious high-density housing at Hulme Crescents in south Manchester. The blocks were constructed in 1972 but quickly deteriorated as the area became blighted by crime. Eventually the city council pulled down the estate just twenty-one years after it was built, amidst a shift in public opinion, particularly about 'streets in the sky'. (Getty Images)

Below left: An ugly, harsh concrete stair tower at the Balfron estate in East London. The rough material and the blocky forms can be thought of as un-natural and de-humanising.

language used by the former camp, along with 'monstrous carbuncle' and 'concrete monstrosity'.

In 2016, the then transport minister, John Hayes, wrote a press release decrying the 'cult of ugliness' in post-war architecture, stating that the bloody-minded brutalists had imposed 'aesthetically worthless' buildings and structures on our towns and cities, and encouraging a return to traditional 'beautiful' architecture, particularly in transport planning. Very little transport architecture is truly brutalist; it is mostly shaped by the efficiencies of engineering and is not architectural at all. This is another example of the emotive words brutal, brutalist, brutalism being misapplied as a catch-all for every dreary concrete structure.

Did you know?

Brutalism's undoing, according to Reyner Banham, was to be seen in 'the innumerable blocks of flats built throughout the world that use the prestige of Le Corbusier's *béton brut* as an excuse for low-cost surface treatment'.

While the futuristic materials and technologies and labour-saving devices of the 1960s implied the end of building maintenance, this was not really so. Even concrete buildings require routine maintenance, and where this was lacking, little understood or later axed through budget-cutting, brutalist buildings suffered. Litter-strewn, graffiti-covered and crumbling buildings look bad and feel intimidating no matter what period they are from, but concrete wastelands and estates that are 'no-go areas' make particularly appealing headlines, justifying to anti-brutalists that this is a failed architecture.

Below left: Forgotten, left-over spaces in twentieth-century architecture often attract anti-social behaviour, and help the fear of crime spread. An area intended as a children's play space here in front of Goldfinger's Trellick Tower has become a graffiti-covered, litter-strewn wasteland. Or has it?

Below right: The massively heavy elevational treatment at Robin Hood Gardens together with the flare-topped, pre-cast concrete boundary wall detail make this residential estate feel more like a maximum security prison than a place to house families.

7
Love It

After decades of neglect and distrust, having fallen from fashion and having been blamed for a whole manner of social ills, and having prompted a shift back towards the comfortable architecture of traditionalism, brutalist buildings for the most part languished in the doldrums. As the end of the twentieth century drew near, naturally a review of its architecture began to take place. High modernism had already been reassessed: from dowdy and out of date to appreciated and revered, the subject of scholarly and critical review, and now widely admired and given its rightful place in the timeline of architectural history. At the turn of the century, the same could not be said, in the public imagination, for the crumbling concrete car park or crime-ridden estates that epitomised brutalism. Concrete was generally still seen as bad, and brutalist a fittingly derogatory epithet. But in the late 1990s a reassessment of architecture from the 1950s to the 1980s – brutalism in particular but also the post-modern movement that had followed – was underway, and voices praising these buildings began to make themselves heard.

Brutalism, in its reverence of 'as found' materials and aesthetic, has often been described as 'anti-beauty'. CPB's Murray Edwards College in Cambridge, particularly the dome of the dining hall and the adjacent fountain court, is certainly beautiful.

Did you know?

Goldfinger's Trellick tower looms large in popular culture. The inspiration behind
J. G. Ballard's 1975 novel *High Rise*, and featuring in Martin Amis' novel *London Fields*,
the tower also pops up in music videos from Blur to Depeche Mode, on album covers
and in countless films and TV shows.

In the early twenty-first century those voices increased. Not just in Britain but around the world, these unlikely, misunderstood, maligned lumps of concrete began to draw a bigger fanbase, and that fanbase began to come together online. The striking forms and volumes of brutalism lend themselves particularly well to photography, which works particularly well online. Perhaps this is part of the reason that the movement gained such a large international following so quickly. The threatening mood of a brutal landscape can be daunting and disconcerting in real life, but as online imagery the atmosphere can be appreciated safely on a screen. Backed up by a handful of young writers and critics, bloggers and photographers who captured the mood of this reversal, as well as by the academic writing of architectural historians, these buildings and their history entered a period of reappraisal. The negative emotive responses are lessening with time; a new appreciation of the movement is surfacing. For a generation who have grown up with the support of a generous welfare state, these buildings and their materials are not threatening, but representative of something important. For the subsequent generation, concrete is as much a part of the background of Britain as thatched cottages – it's just part of the long canon of architecture of the past. You can study, learn from, like or dislike brutalist buildings just as you can from Victorian, Georgian or any other architecture.

To the 'love it' camp, brutalist architecture is the architecture of social freedom. It is representative of a generous welfare state and of ideals of equality. The architecture may initially appear intimidating, but it is a badge of honour to see past that, to appreciate the beauty of the rough concrete, the drama of the composition, and to respect the architectural intimidation. Architecture and planning are not seen as the root of all evil. Instead, it is a lack of maintenance and a lack of understanding that have pigeon-holed these masterpieces and blamed them for all subsequent social ills. The Barbican is held up as an example, a brutalist housing project that works, enriching the lives of its residents. If the Barbican can succeed, with regular, sensitive maintenance, cared for by its users and celebrated, then surely the problems of other so-called 'failed' housing projects cannot be blamed on architecture?

Under threat, brutalism in recent years has become an architectural cause célèbre. Having achieved cult status as the unlovable architecture of the recent past, this underdog movement is now the subject of wide-ranging coffee table books, websites, opinion pieces and campaigns. Achieving the age of over thirty years, these buildings have become eligible for statutory protection through listing. Some of the finest examples have achieved listed status, but many more brutalist masterpieces remain unprotected. Altogether, post-war architecture constitutes a tiny fraction of all of Britain's listed buildings, only around 0.02 per cent.

Publicity-generating campaigns to 'save' various brutalist icons have blazed across the headlines, one after another, throughout the last decade. Their reassessment has been regularly challenged as the anti-brutalists continue to fight their corner. Some campaigns have had success, others have failed. One of the most notable battles played out at Park

The lake terrace, outside the arts centre foyer, at the Barbican estate. The massive scale of the estate is broken down by repetitive detailing, view through, cascading planting and water features.

Hill in Sheffield. Seen as a monstrous eyesore that physically hampered the regeneration of Sheffield city centre, there was significant animosity towards this structure when English Heritage (now Historic England) listed the site in 1998, making it Europe's largest listed building, and spearheaded a campaign to resurrect the megalith. The remaining tenants were relocated, and the refurbishment project began in 2004. The brick infill panels and interiors were stripped out, to be replaced with brightly coloured replacement panels of anodised aluminium. Internal arrangements were modified and updated. Once completed, the flats were then put up for sale on the open market. The reversal of fortunes, from neglected crime hot-spot to desirable urban housing, has not been an entirely smooth process.

The campaign to save the Smithsons' East London housing scheme, Robin Hood Gardens, did not meet with success. Despite a high-profile campaign in the architectural press, the complex was turned down for listing, and has subsequently been approved for demolition. There is no good reason why the structure could not have been refurbished in the same vein as Park Hill; however, the land values and the estate's comparatively low density made it ripe for clearing and replacing with taller, denser dwellings.

Did you know?

Despite demolition, Robin Hood Gardens' importance as an example of brutalist architecture is now enshrined in history, as the Victoria and Albert Museum has acquired a three-storey-high section of the building, including the interior of one flat and a section of walkway, to display alongside their other precious artefacts.

The high-profile signifier that it was socio-economics and perception (rather than architecture) that caused these buildings to be seen as problematic is demonstrated by the pair of estates designed by Erno Goldfinger.

The West London version, the Cheltenham estate, was recognised as an architectural gem in the late 1990s and began to appear on T-shirts, mugs and posters, and in music videos. The prices of the flats (sold by the council to private owners under 'right to buy') went up, reflecting the rising affluence of the area, and a new type of resident began to move in. The East London version, the Brownfield estate, sat in a less desirable part of the city where it was less well recognised and subject to different socio-economic forces. As the Trellick became a popular symbol of the turning fortunes of brutalism, the Balfron and the Brownfield estate languished, forgotten and unloved

Socio-economics have swung around and are now reshaping the Balfron's future. As East London has become a more affluent place, Olympic uplift or otherwise, today the Balfron has been cleared of social tenants and is undergoing a refurbishment, with the flats for sale on the open market, and promoted as a brutalist masterpiece to young, in-the-know investors. The rising and falling fortunes of these buildings are symptomatic of the way brutalism is changing in popular opinion. While it stood empty, awaiting redevelopment, the National Trust dressed one of Balfron's top floor flats as it might have been when first occupied, and offered brutalist-themed walking tours of the estate. Fans of brutalism booked these tours out within days and they proved a huge success, to the great surprise of many of the trust's members and the estate's tenants.

A battle lost was to protect John Madin's Central Library in Birmingham. Prominently and confidently sited in the city centre, whatever else it was it was unavoidable. With its stepped-out upper storeys it loomed, and the steely grey concrete truly glowered, making it very much a brutalist masterpiece. Its fortress-like appearance epitomised knowledge and power. The residents of Birmingham were divided on whether the loss of the Madin library was a good or bad thing.

Below left: A detail of the lift and stair tower glazing at the Balfron Tower, Brownfield estate, by Erno Goldfinger. The narrow slit windows and thick concrete walls reference the details of medieval fortresses.
Below right: A resident surveys an elevation of the Brownfield estate from the concrete link bridge that leads to the community centre.

The Preston bus garage has a more positive story to tell. The building was recommended for listing a number of times, but repeatedly turned down by government ministers. In the end, a campaign by residents demonstrated sufficiently that rather than out-of-touch architectural historians, this was the people of Preston saying loud and clear that they wanted to save their bus station: that it was iconic, identifiable and unique, and deserved to be given a future. It was listed Grade II in 2013 and is currently being redeveloped.

Not all brutalist buildings have had to fight to be appreciated. Some, such as the Barbican complex, have been almost universally accepted from the outset. The UEA have cherished and protected their buildings. Oxford and Cambridge colleges have generally maintained their buildings well. They have been not always understood, but have been respected nonetheless.

The critical reappraisal of brutalism has brought many of the buildings full circle. First lauded, then mistrusted, then hated, neglected, run-down, then reassessed, celebrated and in many cases re-habilitated, now appreciated and widely celebrated. Some are even statutorily protected. Taking their place in architectural history, they now inspire a new generation of designers, free of the shackles of their turbulent past.

A resident of Birmingham poses amidst the partially demolished remains of John Madin's Birmingham Central Library. Is this a sad loss for twentieth-century architecture, or a huge win for Birmingham city centre? Opinion is divided. (Georgina Watts)

Preston bus garage, listed in 2013, is being cleaned up and reinvented. A major new public space is planned where the buses once pulled in, linking the site back to the town. A redeveloped bus station, coach park and multi-storey car park, plus a new home for the Preston Youth Zone, are all part of the ambitious £23.3 million plan by Lancashire County Council.

8
What Now?

Sadly, brutalist buildings are not universally recognised for the important role they have to play in architectural history. Many are unprotected and under threat – while this book was being written, John Madin's Birmingham library was bulldozed, the Smithsons' Robin Hood Gardens are in the process of coming down, Dunelm House at the University of Durham is under threat of demolition, large elements of the Southbank Centre are unprotected and subject to commercial pressures, and the striking St Peter's Seminary in Cardross, Scotland, languishes as a ruin.

But there is hope! As brutalism becomes increasingly popular, so a greater understanding ensues. The Preston bus garage was turned down for listed status twice before being granted protection through Grade II listed status. The structure is now subject to a competition to refurbish and revitalise it as a community asset.

Anyone can apply for a building to become listed, so unlisted brutalist buildings that you care about could be a candidate for listing. Contact Historic England listing teams in your local area for further information and advice.

With a boom in urban development in the UK over the last few years, a large number of amorphous, concrete buildings are springing up. Is this neo-brutalism?

Dunelm House at the University of Durham. This threatened building divides opinion. (Kath Fall)

Campaigning can make a big difference! This is why the single most valuable thing you can do next is join the Twentieth Century Society, and add your weight to their ongoing campaigns for twentieth-century architecture across Britain (https://c20society.org.uk/). The society not only campaign, they also run an excellent series of talks, walks, debates and events focused on twentieth-century architecture in Britain. Their website and regular magazine are interesting and informative, and make the society well worth joining.

Local campaign groups can also make a big difference – if there isn't one that covers your favourite local brutalist building, start one! Lots of help and advice is out there, from the Architectural Heritage Fund (http://ahfund.org.uk/) to Historic England's Local Engagement Advisors (https://historicengland.org.uk/advice/planning/local-heritage/).

Blogs and online resources

The Brutalism Appreciation Society on Facebook is a large and active group, numbering 44,000 members sharing images of and discussing brutalist architecture internationally.

Instagram also has a great number of brutalism accounts, which are perfect for discovering images and stories of brutal buildings from far and wide.

#SOSBRUTALISM (www.sosbrutalism.org) is a growing online database currently containing over 900 brutalist buildings. It is also a campaign platform, organising exhibitions and particularly highlighting brutalist buildings that are under threat.

Brutalism Online (www.brutalism.online) is a large online resource featuring brutalist buildings from across the world, with a particularly helpful 'buildings list'.

Into the 1970s, what is known as Late Modernism was a diverse time for architecture. Many later buildings share qualities of form, design and material with brutalism; for example, here at Swansea Civic Centre it is clear to see the legacy of Brutalism.

Books

Harwood, Elain, *Space, Hope and Brutalism 1945–1975* (Paul Mellon Centre for Studies in British Art 2015). This is the seminal text on the period that covers brutalism, offering an unparalleled overview of post-war English architecture, setting brutalism within the wider architectural context. Structured around building types, this scholarly book carefully knits architecture, social history, politics and economics to understand and explain post-war architecture.

Franklin, Geraint, *Howell, Killick, Partridge and Amis* (Historic England/RIBA Publishing 2017). Part of a series of books on individual practices, this insightful volume showcases one of the most prolific and important architectural firms working in the mid-twentieth century.

Harwood, Elain, *Chamberlin, Powell and Bon* (RIBA Publishing 2011). Part of the same series as above, this book benefits from fantastic research, and recognises some of the best buildings of the 1960s by this important practice.

Curtis, William J. R., *Denys Lasdun: Architecture, City, Landscape* (Phaidon 1999). Curtis comprehensively assesses Ladsun's work through detailed analysis and a wonderful collection of images, many from the architect's own archive.

Hopkins, Owen, *Lost Futures: The Disappearing Architecture of Post-War Britain* (RA 2017). Hopkins has published a number of interesting books and essays on architecture. This book features thirty-five post-war British buildings, understanding how they came to be built, and highlighting the threats they face.

English Heritage, *Practical Building Conservation: Concrete* (Ashgate/Routledge 2013). Practical Building Conservation is a ten-part series that looks at the conservation of building materials and systems. The edition on concrete is the best resource for understanding the history, application, method and maintenance of the material.

Calder, Barnabas, *Raw Concrete: The Beauty of Brutalism* (2016). This is an excellent, well-researched study that provides an insight into the author's personal journey, from mistrusting and disliking concrete buildings to appreciating the subtlety and complexity of their design.

Places to visit

Many brutalist buildings are public buildings and can be visited free of charge. Some university campuses and Cambridge or Oxford colleges can be visited, but it is worth checking with the institution first. Photography may also be restricted in this type of building, so again this is worth checking before visiting. Some private buildings, including the Hunstanton School, are not generally available to visit.

Heritage Open Days (https://www.heritageopendays.org.uk) and similar events across the country provide the opportunity to get inside some otherwise inaccessible buildings, and co-ordinate tours and events. These are well worth booking. Buildings such as the Royal College of Physicians usually offer tours during London Open House Weekend (http://openhouselondon.org.uk), giving the opportunity to get up close with a building normally not open to the public.

Organisations such as the National Trust and the Royal Academy have in the past held exhibitions and events on the subject of brutalism, so keep an eye out for more of these in the future.

Concrete, we love it.